GoD is very holy

by Denise Vezey

Illustrated by Victoria Ponikvar-Frazier

Equipping Kids for Life!

A Faith Parenting Guide can be found on page 32.

Dedication:

In memory of my grandmother, Ella Sprague

Faith Kids® is an imprint of
Cook Communications Ministries, Colorado Springs, CO 80918
Cook Communications, Paris, Ontario
Kingsway Communications, Eastbourne, England

GOD IS VERY HOLY
© 2001 by Denise Vezey for text and Victoria Ponikvar-Frazier for illustrations

Edited by Jeannie Harmon
Designed by Sonya Design and Illustration

Printed in Canada
05 04 30 02 01   5 4 3 2

ISBN 0-7814-3504-8

99-17033
CIP

Table of Contents

My very best book

Guess what?

I have a new comic book!

It's filled with pictures

and lots of action.

There are bright colors and only a few words.

What a great way to spend the day!

I look, I laugh, I smile.
I read, then rest awhile.

I love to read
my many books
about spaceships and lions,
heroes and crooks!

After I read the comics,

I get out my books on outer space.

I can fly my own space ship!

Watch out moon! Here I come!

I'm Captain Zoom!

Mom calls me. *Crash!*
I come back to earth.
"Could you please find your Bible?"
My *Bible?*
Uh-oh. I better dig through this mess.

"Is this it?" Mom asks.

I nod my head yes.

"Honey, did you know
the Bible is the only book
in the whole world
filled with God's words?

"Think of the Bible as a letter from God.
He tells us exciting stories
about all kinds of people
and places we've never seen.

"Since every word comes from God,
each story in it is true.
And because God is holy,
His words are holy too.
That's why we need to
treat our Bibles with care."

"I see, Mommy.
I won't throw my Bible
on the ground,
or pile other books on top of it.
I won't step on it,
or draw all over the pages."

I look, I laugh, I smile.
I read God's Word a while.

God only gave us
one holy book.
I'll take care of the Bible,
my very best book!

My time to be brave

One day on the playground,
the big boys got mad.
Two of them wanted our football.
They said God's name
in a very bad way.

I look, I skid, I stop!
I shake my head, I'm shocked!

God's name is holy—
a word shining bright.
If we want to speak it,
we must use it right!

They shouldn't say
God's name that way.
Not in front of me!
My mom and dad told me
God's name is *holy*.
It's like a prayer.

We don't call our cat, "God."
And we never say God's name
when we are angry.
So, I take a deep breath,
and walk over to the boys.

Joey is screaming,
"It's our ball!"
"Yeah, give it to us!" Paul yells.
"Stop it!" I say. "We need to talk."
Uh-oh. Now I'm in trouble.

They look right at me.

"Stay out of this. We don't need you."

"Yeah, you're nothing but a small fry."

"Hey, you guys," I shout back,

"I don't care about the football."

Joey and Paul look surprised.

"Don't you know
God is bigger than you!
He is greater than you!
He could squash you like a bug
for saying His name that way!
But He won't. He loves you too much."

All the boys got very quiet.
Then one of them said,
"You're pretty smart for a little guy.
We'll try and watch what we say."
I smiled, then threw the
football as hard as I could.

I run, I kick the ball.
It flies, right over the wall!

God's name is holy—
a word shining bright.
If we want to speak it,
we must use it right.

My grumpy Sunday

Today is Sunday.

We always rush around to get ready.

I have to dress up

in pants and a shirt I don't even like!

Then we go and SIT in church.

Why are Sundays like this?

I fuss, I fume, I whine.
I scrub until I shine.

The rest of the week
I run or I play.
Why are my Sundays
always this way?

I decide to ask my dad.
"Why do we go to church?
Sundays are my only day to sleep in!
Can't we just stay home
and eat pancakes?"

"You don't sound very happy today."

"I'm not," I reply.

Daddy takes my hand and says,

"Let's go eat some pancakes.

"Maybe you would
like Sundays better
if you knew why
they are special to God.

"You see, a long time ago,
it only took God six days
to make the whole earth!
But it was a lot of work.
He rested when it was done.

"Then He made one day
each week for us to rest
and thank Him for all He has done.
We go to church to sing happy songs
and praise Him for His love."

We drive to church.
I think about what my dad said.
We sing and I feel good inside.
When we bow our heads to pray,
I think of God
and everyone I love.

I eat, I sing, I pray.
I laugh, I learn, I play.

There's one special day
for worship and rest.
We thank God and praise Him
'cause He is the best!

Dear God, please help me to treat You with respect, for You are very holy. Amen.

"There is no one holy like the Lord."
1 Samuel 2:2 (NIV)

God Is Very Holy

Age: 4-7

Life Issue: To understand that because God is holy,
we need to show respect for God and His Word.

Spiritual Building Block: Respect

Learning Styles
Help your children learn about respect in the following ways:

Sight: With your children, walk around your house and find all of the
Bibles. As in the story, were they in special places or were they under
papers and hidden from view? Talk to your children about showing respect
for God's Word and agree together that the Bible will be well cared for in
your house.

Sound: Sometimes people say words that hurt. When they use God's
name in an inappropriate way, it must hurt God. Read Exodus 20:7 to
your children and talk about what the Bible says about misusing God's name.
Memorize one of the following verses together: Psalm 111:9b; 135:1a; 145:1b.

Touch: What are some ways that we show respect for God? Do we obey
what He tells us to do in His Word? Do we honor our moms and dads?
Do we talk respectfully about God, the Bible, and the church? Talk to your
children about showing love to God by respecting Him in their everyday life.
Pray with your children, thanking God for what He has given us to enjoy.